MICROCIRCUITS, SOCIETY AND E

Occasional Paper 8

Microcircuits, Society and Education

W Gosling
Professor, Head of the School of Electrical
Engineering at the University of Bath

Council for Educational Technology
for the United Kingdom

Published and distributed by the
Council for Educational Technology
3 Devonshire Street, London W1N 2BA

© Council for Educational Technology 1978

First published 1978
ISBN 0 902204-86-6
ISSN 0307-952X

Other than as permitted under the Copyright Act 1956, no part of this publication may be photo-copied, recorded, or otherwise reproduced, stored in a retrieval system or transmitted in any form by any electronic or mechanical means without the prior permission of the copyright owner.

 British Library Cataloguing in Publication Data

Gosling, William
Microcircuits, society and education. – (Council for Educational Technology for the United Kingdom.
Occasional papers; 8; 0307-952X)
1. Integrated circuits – Social aspects
I. Title II. Series
301.24'3 TK7874
ISBN 0-902204-86-6

Printed in Great Britain by
Direct Design (Bournemouth) Ltd,
Sturminster Newton, Dorset,
DT10 1AZ

List of illustrations

Figure	Page

1: Each new advance in electronics is identified here by the name or initials of the new process. As the years pass, the delay each circuit introduces gets shorter and shorter.   19

2: As the circuits get faster it also becomes possible to get more and more into each square millimeter of chip, but the cost of each square millimetre falls.   19

3: The year-by-year increase in number of devices per silicon chip is awe-inspiring. One million per chip looks likely in the eighties.   20

4: Complexity is not bought at high cost — indeed, as complexity increases costs fall.   20

5: (a) The Ferranti microcomputers type F100-L: a 16-bit bipolar chip only 0.23in square which will (b) pass through the eye of a needle. (Photographs by permission of Ferranti Ltd.)   23

6: A modern read-only memory (ROM) on a silicon chip only a few millimetres square. (Photograph by permission of Mullard Ltd.)   26

7: Transition of information over glass fibres like these (in the form of pulses of light) may render conventional cables obsolete for many purposes. A cable only 7mm in diameter consisting of four pairs of optical fibres and a central strength member can carry 7860 simultaneous conversations. The much larger diameter, 4800-pair cable (left) can carry 4800 conversations, and the similarly-sized 18-tube coaxial cable (top) can carry 10,800 conversations on each pair of tubes on the latest 60 MHz system. (Photograph by permission of Standard Telephones and Cables Ltd.)   26

8: A word processor is likely to change profoundly education, clerical work, and creative writing. The Philips WP5001 range links the typewriter keyboard with a visual display unit allowing immediate presentation of typed information. A microprocessor offers correction of text and adjustment in layout before commitment to paper. (Photograph by permission of Philips Business Equipment Division, and supplied by Good Relations Ltd.)   34

Foreword

This essay has its origins in a talk Professor Gosling gave to the second biennial meeting of the 'Participating Bodies' of the Council for Educational Technology — a diverse collection of organizations who are interested in collaborating with the Council.

In retrospect I can see three good reasons why Professor Gosling's name occurred to me as a speaker, why I was delighted when he accepted our invitation, and why I was not in the least surprised when his stimulating and provocative talk fired those present and led to an afternoon of outstandingly thoughtful discussion. First, he is a leading authority on electronics and particularly on microelectronics; second, he has an outstanding sensitivity to the social implications of technological change; and third, he can express his insights, whether in written or spoken form, with a clarity which renders them immediately comprehensible to a non-technical audience.

The question might be asked, particularly by those most aware of the Council's insistence that educational technology is a matter of a systematic approach to teaching and learning not necessarily related to the employment of technological means and equipment, whether this particular topic is of central importance to the Council. It is, by general admission, of central importance to our society. The probability that microelectronics will herald a new industrial revolution is now (but only in the last few months) an accepted topic for discussion, if not yet a contemporary dogma. But how is it of particular relevance to education and training, and more particularly to the Council for Educational Technology?

Primarily, I would suggest, in terms of the nature of the social change implied, the crucial part which education and training may have to play in helping is to adapt to that change. Professor Gosling emphasizes that the ultimate shape of society, as a result of these changes, is highly speculative; any prophecies must be tentative in the extreme. But what we see happening today shows us where our path is likely to lead in the short term: to the replacement of traditional industries with a relatively large labour force by new industries based on microelectronics. These new industries will employ much smaller numbers of people, at a much more highly skilled and qualified level.

What happens then depends on how, collectively, we react. If we manage to rise above the minimal level of stupidity which is necessary for the survival of our society in any tolerable form, then as I see it we shall have most pressing need for education and training. We shall need vocational training and retraining, often in new skills. We shall need continuing and recurrent education in the broadest sense, in terms of both range of content and ease of availability, as an important element in all individuals' pattern of life. This will be necessary both as a socially acceptable way of filling time not spent at work, and as a way of maintaining self-esteem in the absence of employment.

But there is another aspect. If the social consequences of microelectronics may face us with heavy additional demands for education and training, the technological potential offers education and training great opportunities. For CET, the challenge is to identify these opportunities, particularly in the application to education and training of the new systems and techniques which are emerging. We are particularly concerned to recognize such applications, and to ensure that the new technologies come in to education and training (for come they will) as appropriate ways to meet real needs and not in the classic form of a solution looking for a problem.

For these reasons alone this essay is of central importance to any discussion of the future of education and training and hence of the role of the Council. But apart altogether from its relevance to the Council and its work, it is in my view an outstanding contribution to a vital contemporary debate. The Council is happy to be instrumental in bringing it before a wider audience.

I should like to add my personal thanks to Professor Gosling for agreeing to talk to the Participating Bodies Conference, for agreeing that the Council should publish his talk, and for producing the text with exemplary speed. It is always the busiest people who deliver on time!

G Hubbard — Director
Council for Educational Technology
for the United Kingdom

The Kingdom of Sand

My purpose is to try to look at the problem of education — that perpetual problem from which no generation will ever be wholly released — and I shall take the particular standpoint of somebody who, by an accident of personal history, is in a good position to see something of the quite incredible discontinuity in the nature of our society which is just beginning.

To talk about a discontinuity in our social patterns may sound unduly alarmist, and indeed at once one must hurry to add that even in the biggest of changes many things go on as before. People, after all, are still people. Yet we would deceive ourselves sadly if we did not begin by acknowledging that we find ourselves on the threshold now of something more significant and more far-reaching in its consequences than perhaps anything that has happened to our race since our long-dead ancestors took fire into their service. I shall seek to demonstrate the truth of this unlikely statement later — for the moment let me simply state what I believe, that the microelectronics revolution, bringing with it the certainty of thinking machines of more than biological complexity, is the culmination and climax of the industrial and scientific revolution which has gripped and shaken the human world for the last three hundred years.

No aspect of human life is likely to remain wholly unaffected by this remarkable development, least of all education, by its nature preoccupied with that very business of storing, retrieving and disseminating information upon which the microelectronics age will have its most immediate and rapid impact. Educationists, then, should be thinking and debating what the likely consequences of this revolutionary change will be for them, and it is to this debate that I seek to make a contribution.

The easiest way for me to do that, and the way most certain of success, would be to concentrate on the coming hardware, the new equipment — toys, some might say — with which we shall face our tasks. It would be straightforward to describe data retrieval systems in the home, word processors, facsimile transmission, computers, interpersonal communication, archival stores; and to do so would be neither facile nor irrelevant: coming to terms with these new artefacts, their potential and consequences, is an important task ahead of us and one which we must not shirk. Even so, that is not the task to which I propose now to address myself.

To perceive the nature of these new products of a new age is hardly enough, for we can be aware of them yet not aware of their total consequences. At this stage, when the game is barely begun, it is an overall impression of trends and implications which is of the greatest value. Although it might be gathered by considering a mass of independent possibilities and hoping that taken together they would cause some synthesis to appear, this does not seem the most direct way.

Instead, I feel it more useful to try to look beyond the immediate technical developments, which anyway evolve so rapidly, trying instead to form an overview of the character of our age. We must strive to see it in evolution, not, that is, only as state but also as process. Success in this task would not only be a matter of perceiving what is now possible or must certainly soon come to be, but also of identifying directly those trends and tendencies, about the working out of which it is impossible as yet to be certain, but which can inform, regulate and guide our conjectures as to what the future may hold.

Further, as educationists we must be concerned with that future in two important aspects. It is true beyond question that we must be much concerned with the way in which the unfolding technology causes us to go about our work. The very means of going about the educational process, the equipment that we use and the ways in which we deploy it, are going to be profoundly transformed.

I must affirm most clearly the importance of this aspect of our concerns. But the other facet is no less important and it is this: we need to recognize that the coming change in our world is going to modify not only the means by which education is carried on but also the very ends at which it aims.

If we do not try just as hard to identify the likely path of evolution in ends as well as means, we shall go far astray. It is to this ambitious dual task that I propose we should, for a while, direct our thoughts.

Evidently, in the short space available here, subjects of this magnitude can be opened but little more. One could only be conclusive at the cost of being glib. Yet let us do what we can.

What indeed is this change in the world that we now have to prepare for? Electronics has, after all, already had a major impact on all our lives through developments, first in broadcasting, then communications generally; in automation; and in computers. Its penetration into all fields of human activity has been swift wherever the ability of electronics to enhance human senses and memory could be significant. To be sure, cost has held back the scope of its application, as also has the limit on complexity to which electronic artefacts could reasonably go. Reliability has exercised some restraint: it is no good building a complex system if the frequency with which it breaks down is such that its utility is destroyed. What we are now grappling with is radical precisely because it presents a technological change in the way of building electronics which reduces the cost by a factor of at least a thousand — perhaps more — and improves its reliability so greatly that failure rates are no longer an effective limitation on system complexity.

Until the sixties, electronic equipment was built pretty much in the style established in the nineteenth century for electrical scientific instruments. The various electrical devices — transistors, resistors, capacitors and so on — were independently fabricated, then assembled on a board or chassis used as a mechanical support, and wired together by hand. This changed out of recognition with the evolution of microcircuit technology in the sixties. By a photographic process — descended both from the photolithographic processes used in high quality printing and from the microphotography developed for compact archival document records — the electronic circuits were created on the surface of a fragment of monocrystalline silicon. Such circuits could immediately be fabricated in hundreds or thousands at a time, at low cost, and because the circuit is virtually 'buried' in the surface of a solid inert silicon crystal it is almost indestructible in ordinary use and very long lived. Freed from limitations of cost and reliability electronics can now take off. Applications which were potential become immediately actual.

The first consequence to be seen by ordinary people was the electronic calculator which, within a few months, doomed the mechanical calculator to extinction and, more strikingly, led millions throughout the world to regard a calculator as a normal part of their personal equipment — people who would not conceivably have purchased the same capability in mechnical form. Something similar happened in the case of the electronic watch, which is killing its mechanical competitor, although in this case the market expansion is not so striking.

What is it, then, that gives the new electronics this power to sweep away old artefacts in a remarkably short time — to destroy a flourishing industry in six months or a year and replace it by another quite different in character? Simply: it is the magnitude of the advances involved. We are not concerned here, as in so many other contexts, with a new technique which is just marginally better than the old, giving a few per cent advantage. In the case of microelectronics, even its first inept applications are ten times cheaper or ten times better, or both, than the technology it replaces.

There is much discussion among sociologists about the so-called technological imperative: are technically possible solutions to problems inevitably always exploited, or can their implementation be resisted by social forces? Because it is hard to make such discussions quantitative, they are inclined to be inconclusive. Opinion tends to the view that there is indeed a technological imperative, but that it is not irresistible. However, if we could but put numbers into the debate, no doubt we would try to measure both the strength of conservative forces within society and also the power of the forces for change. No barrier can be of infinite strength, and we may reasonably presume that success of resistance to change will depend upon the impact that must be withstood. Perhaps the most graphic example of the struggle against new technology and its collapse which comes to mind is the entry of Western technology into Japan in the mid-nineteenth century.

A self-consciously conservative society, Japan, under the Tokugawa Shogunate, had excluded Western artefacts. In particular, firearms were prohibited, because of fears, in the event proved wholly justified, that the introduction of this weapon technology would destroy much that those who controlled the destiny of the country deeply valued. It was, historically, perfectly possible to exclude seventeenth-century Western technology (and the Christian ideology that went with it) because superior though it was, the margin of its advantage was not too great and the indigenous culture therefore could still resist. By the mid-nineteenth century the margin was immeasurably larger. The technological imperative was then so much greater that once American steam warships had demonstrated the power of their guns in Tokyo harbour, no magic the Shogun might summon could save Japan as it was.

That the instrument of transition to being a modern scientific and industrial power was, for the Japanese, the Meiji restoration, that is the nominal restitution of an archaic imperial rule which had not been effective for hundreds of years, is a fascinating, but for present purposes, irrelevant phenomenon of Japanese society. This at least may be said: it satisfied an impulse to conservatism by making it possible for the Daimyo (the leading families) to dominate the new society, as they had dominated the old.

In the whole developed world we are now in something of the situation that Japan experienced when the US commander's black ships were first sighted off her coast. Great change is at hand: that we know. There will be some who argue that we can resist and ignore it, but they will be of no more account than the heirs of the Tokugawas, withdrawing to their hopeless last battle in Nagasaki castle. The future is not theirs and romantic gestures of forlorn conservatism deprive those who make them of any power to shape what is to be. Before we can influence the world to come, at least we must acknowledge its existence, hard though it may be to be certain yet of the outlines which it will take.

We must begin by looking at those pointers which are now to hand. Let us look at the technology itself. We can identify certain of its critical parameters: speed of operation, complexity and cost. Speed and power consumption are related, for we can usually make an electronic circuit work faster by using more power to operate it. What we are concerned with, then, is time taken for a basic circuit operation at a fixed power level. This shows a steady downwards trend. (Figure 1)

In modern electronics our unit of time is not the second, nor yet the microsecond (which is one millionth of a second) but the nanosecond — one thousand of a millionth of a second. To get an impression of what this means, you will perhaps recall that the speed of light is 186,000 miles per second. In a nanosecond light thus travels about one foot. At present our simplest electronic circuits — we call them 'gates' — have operated experimentally in a fraction of a nanosecond: production devices typically operate in about ten nanoseconds. Thus the twinkling of an eye, that metaphor for an irreducibly short interval of time in human terms, and which in fact takes about one tenth of a second, it still time enough for over ten million of these primitive electronic operations, even with our present-day circuits.

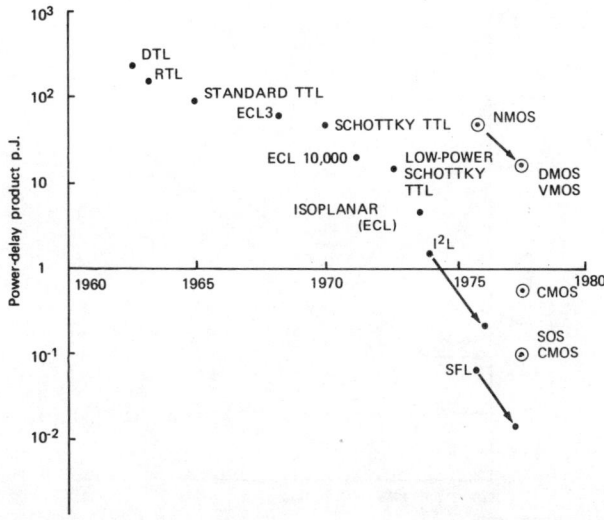

Figure 1: Each new advance in electronics is identified here by the name or initials of the new process. As the years pass, the delay each circuit introduces gets shorter and shorter.

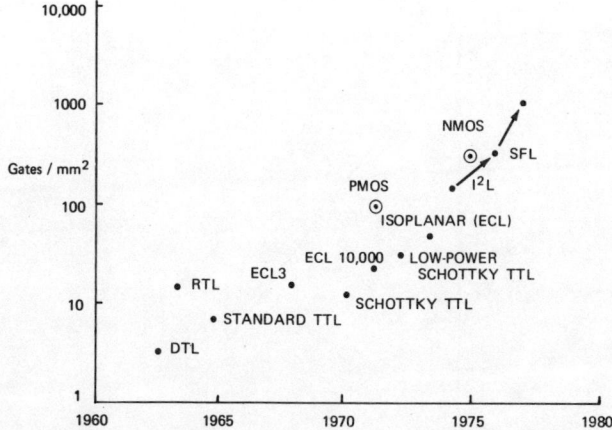

Figure 2: As the circuits get faster it also becomes possible to get more and more into each square millimetre of chip, but the cost of each square millimetre falls.

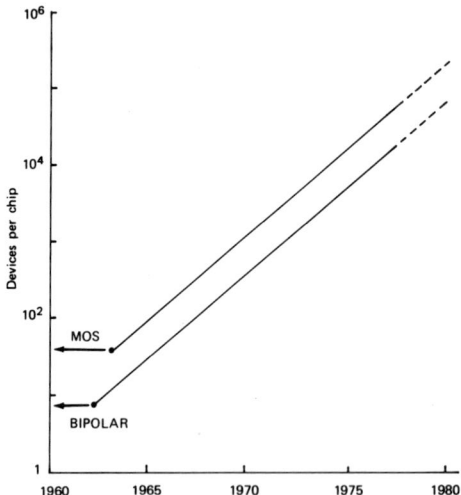

Figure 3: The year-by-year increase in number of devices per silicon chip is awe-inspiring. One million per chip looks likely in the eighties.

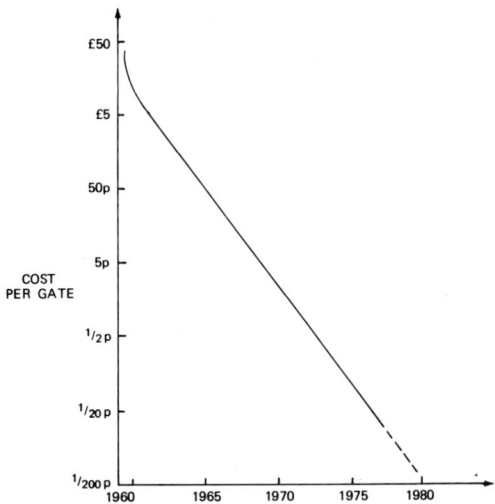

Figure 4: Complexity is not bought at high cost – indeed, as complexity increases costs fall.

Along with increasing speed goes growth in complexity. How many of these simple devices can our circuits combine together? The earliest microcircuits had ten of them, later one hundred, then one thousand, and as a very few years roll by numerical milestone after milestone is passed. (Figure 2) Before the eighties are far run there can be little doubt that we shall see one million electronic gates on a silicon chip only one centimetre square. (Figure 3) On this basis, we could put five hundred distinct devices on the head of a pin. The density of packing already exceeds the density of packing of cells in the brain. In speed and complexity the natural world has already been surpassed: we are not building machines of biological complexity, we are building machines of a complexity of detail which biological evolution has never achieved, except, if you like, through our own agency. And these microcircuits are cheap — almost immeasurably cheap — to make. As speed and complexity increase, cost tumbles, and no less dramatically. (Figure 4)

I myself first learned to programme a computer a little over twenty years ago. The machine was called Pegasus — in its day a triumph of engineering of which Ferranti were justifiably proud. It filled a room the size of an average sitting room and was rather unpleasant to work with in summer, because it used so much power that the room got uncomfortably warm. The engineers serviced it for three hours every day, and it was then 90% probable that it would continue to work for the remaining twenty-one. Today I carry on my belt a computer which is rather more powerful, has never been serviced since the day it arrived (and with luck never will be) and takes rather less power than a pocket electric torch. More to the point, the Pegasus installation of a quarter-century ago cost £50,000, whereas today's counterpart cost just over £300; and we all know what has happened to the pound in your pocket in the meantime. We are moving to the situation where the cost of an electronic device is the cost of the case that contains it, of the keyboard which actuates it, of the displays, the batteries, anything in fact but the electronics itself. (Figure 5)

A technological change so profound spawns others, which support it and are in turn made practicable by it. I will name just the two most important for our present concerns, although there are many others. Because microelectronics makes the processing and manipulation of information in all its many forms so cheap and effective, it calls for two more innovations, above all others: namely, cheap means of storing information and cheap means of transmitting it over long distances.

As to the former — the memory function of our new intelligent machines — microelectronics partly itself provides the answer. Semiconductor microelectronic stores fabricated on silicon chips are now replacing all others, at least in those applications where access to the information is required in a hundred nanoseconds or so. These devices, called RAMs (random access memories) and ROMs (read-only memories), are the basic tool of modern microcomputer design. (Figure 6) To say more, we must define the way in which the properties of

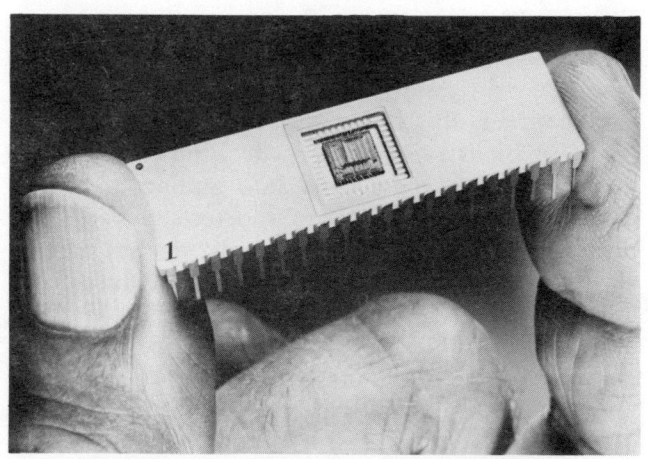

Figure 5: (a) The Ferranti microcomputer type F100-L: a chip of formidable complexity which (b) nevertheless, will pass through the eye of a (rather large) needle. (Photographs reproduced by permission of Ferranti Ltd.)

these artificial memories are described. Their access time I have already mentioned — it is quoted in nanoseconds. As to their extent, how much they can contain, this is measured in binary digits, or 'bits'. A bit is a single yes-no decision between two equiprobable choices. Any information at all can be expressed as a longer or shorter series of these decisions, as is done, for example, in the game of Twenty Questions. To give a feel for just what a bit corresponds to in everyday terms, a longish novel of 100,000 words may be encoded in about two-and-a-half million bits, or two-and-a-half megabits, in the jargon. Marcel Proust's great work, *La Recherche du Temps Perdu,* at four million words is perhaps one hundred megabits. The ideas presented here — about the same length as a paper in a learned journal — correspond to some one hundred and fifty thousand bits (or 150 kilobits), if one takes into account only the overt content and ignores the information which may additionally be conveyed by the particular style in which it is presented.

Electronic stores, of different kinds, in practical use show a kind of 'trade-off' between capacity and access time. The RAMs, for example, give back stored information in the time that it would take light to travel from one end to another of a cricket pitch, but their content is relatively small, typically no more than could be spoken in ten or twenty minutes. By contrast a magnetic tape can be used to form a store — it would be called an archival store — big enough to contain all that Proust ever wrote, but taking as much as a second to deliver up any particular item of information that it contains.

Most recently of all, using the technique of optical holograms, an even newer kind of archival store is in process of being born. It looks as though this will have a capacity up to perhaps one million megabits, corresponding to a library of four hundred thousand volumes in book form, but stored in something the size of a television set and with each item of information accessible in about one second. The cost of such a store is likely to be much less than one hundred-thousandth part of a penny for every bit stored — perhaps as little as five pence per megabit. This would mean that the cost of storing a long novel this way would be about 12½ pence, and the whole of Proust could be held in the memory for perhaps £5.

With storage capabilities like this in prospect it is at least arguable that our civilization may cease to be a paper-based one, as it now is. However that may be, the skills of reading and writing will not become obsolete, as some propose. The written word will still be the most efficient means of communication between people and machines for the foreseeable future.

Another invention which modern electronics has stolen from time's dragon hoard is the optical fibre. By converting information into inconceivably fleeting pulses of light, it becomes feasible to transmit them over vast distances using hair-like fibres of very special glass which trap the light within themselves and carry it almost without loss. Glass, like the silicon of which microcircuits are made, comes from sand — of which there is an inexhaustible supply — and very little goes to make

Figure 6: A modern read-only memory (ROM) on a silicon chip only a few millimetres square. (Photograph reproduced by permission of Mullard Ltd.)

Figure 7: Transmission of information over glass fibres like these (in the form of pulses of light) may render conventional cables obsolete for many purposes. (Photograph reproduced by permission of Standard Telephones and Cables Ltd.)

an optical fibre which can carry an enormous flow of information — at present such a fibre can easily carry a megabit per second, and potentially its capacity is much more. The optical fibre will replace both cables and telephone wires, making it possible to channel right into our homes, schools, and universities a flow of information greater by far than would have been possible or economic with existing cable technology. The world of the future will be held together by a fine-spun web of glass, fragile yet immeasurably connective.

Nobody knows what the combined impact of all this technology will ultimately be, but we can begin to discern its impact on industry, and hence on the employment prospects of those whose education is our charge. At present the 'take-up' of the new technology is very uneven. Some industries, like computers and communications, have proved to be relatively very open to it, whilst others — the great unwashed, the traditional and the dormant — exploit it far less. We see the consequences in their growth patterns. There is probably no industry which, in the end, the new technology will not affect, revolutionizing production processes and organization of the firm, even if not of the product. But so far those which have been open and able to absorb it have shown startling and unmatched growth, whilst the others have languished. It is also noteworthy how employment patterns within the industries which have embraced the new technology compare with those which have yet to do so. In the electronics-oriented activities, the staff count per pound of wealth generated has fallen sharply. Whereas a worker in ordinary manufacturing industry does well to generate more than £10,000 in added value per year, a young man designing microcircuits is expected by his employers to generate no less than thirty times as much. Thus for an equal generation of wealth, far fewer people will be needed.

Not only will the employees be fewer, their distribution between jobs will be very different. The future-oriented companies show a much higher proportion of their staffs, amounting to an outright majority in some cases, in managerial, marketing, design and higher technical roles, and a smaller proportion in semi-skilled, unskilled and routine tasks. This applies no less to white collar than manual areas of employment: the office as well as the workshop is ripe for depletion.

Of the political and social consequences of this change there is much to be said. In the eighteenth century some 90% of the British population were engaged in agriculture. By the late twentieth century only 5% are so employed, yet the level of agricultural production is more than tenfold greater. Had this fall in agricultural employment been foreseen it might have appeared a disaster: what would the unemployed agricultural labourer do? We are the descendants of those farming people. Both the concepts with which we are here concerned and the lives we ourselves lead would have been incomprehensible to them. Perhaps that is part of the answer.

Early in the twentieth century about 70% of our population was employed, one way or another, in manufacturing industry. That proportion has already fallen by this present date, to about 40%. The technology now to come will reduce the fraction to 10%, perhaps 5%, with increased product. It would be natural to fear this change, even to seek to oppose it. Before we do so, however, let us ask ourselves two questions: first, would we like to return to the hard lives of eighteenth-century agricultural labourers, and secondly, is it likely that our descendants, one hundred years from now, would really prefer to return to the lives of twentieth-century assembly line workers? If the answer to both of these questions is no, we must address ourselves to the problem of applying the new technology, not evading it.

So far as educationists are concerned, the conclusion that we draw is that in future few of our children will need to be prepared for a working life in manufacturing industry, but those few will need very high order skills. It is likely that future industrial employment will be for graduates, technicians, skilled craftsmen, and few others. Mass production and repetitive tasks of all kinds will be best done by robots.

The professions are also likely to be profoundly influenced. To take the example of medicine, one of the most highly prized professional skills at the present time is that of accurate diagnosis. A lifetime of hard-won experience enables the medical specialist to put together the signs and symptoms that the patient exhibits into a significant clinical picture. However, it is just this kind of information retrieval task which the computer does exceptionally well. Provided that a reasonably competent medical pracitioner is available to read signs and symptoms and communicate them to the machine, the diagnostic skill of the very best human specialists can remain trapped and available in the computer store at negligible cost. On the other hand and by contrast, there are some tasks which will, perhaps, never be automated. Surgery seems a very unpromising field (although anaesthesia is not, and even the surgeon will have many automatic equipments and instruments at his disposal). Equally, it is hard to conceive of a robot nurse or psychotherapist, because these are necessarily fields where human contact is the essence of the task.

It would be possible to go on: in law, engineering, architecture, changes there must be. Jobs will disappear and others gain new importance, and the outcome will bear little relationship to the status and esteem in which the same jobs are held at the present time. Only a seer could predict the whole pattern, yet paradoxically in education we must prepare for it. All we can do is cling to the belief that now, more than ever in history, we must be flexible not only in our educational methods but even in goals. We must ever be prepared to devise new kinds of educational experiences and abandon old ones. Above all we must avoid the adoption of organizational structures or, and this is particularly important, educational technologies which tend to congeal patterns of teaching and learning into forms not easily changed.

So much for ends: what are the implications for the methods which we shall adopt? The educational process already has many varied forms. It can, for example, work for those who study privately, with no supervision of any kind, if they are well enough motivated. The Open University has brilliantly demonstrated how an institutional framework can be supportive to a home student, greatly increasing his chances of success with what, by conventional standards, is minimal personal contact with those who teach him. At the same time, conventional university and polytechnic courses continue to look like the broad educational highway for the majority of students.

You will have heard predictions that the development of modern means of information storage, processing and transmission will make obsolete the conventional higher education institutions derived from the mediæval need for face-to-face confrontation. There are those willing to predict that all teaching will be in the student's home using stored or transmitted material. In my opinion, this is naive: it neglects profound psychological and sociological realities about human beings which are no less compelling than the technological imperatives. The schools and universities are social structures for learning and provide psychological mechanisms conducive to that end. If it were not so, the lecture would never have survived the cheap availability of printed books.

It seems far more plausible to suppose that institutions will continue to exist and that the new technology will augment, expand and supplement their roles. I believe that this is the true lesson to be drawn from the success of the Open University. The fact is that it still is, for its students, a true university based on interpersonal contacts with tutors, counsellors, and, in the summer schools, lecturers. What radio and television technology has done is to diminish the formerly irreducible minimum extent of that contact, and some of its senior members would certainly argue that good printed books and course material have been even more significant in that respect than broadcasting.

To talk of books is to come to the core of the matter: we have to admit that the invention of writing and later the printing press were the advances in educational technology to which even now with all that has come since, we unquestionably owe most. The scholar is still the man of letters and the written word his tool. It is, so I believe, in this very area that the most dramatic changes are likely to come.

This paper was first written with a ballpoint pen on a pad, corrected, then typed by my secretary. I might perhaps have recorded it on tape instead, but being a scientist and therefore frequently having to incorporate mathematical symbolism in my output, I have not taken to the tape recorder as much as my arts colleagues have. It is unlikely that either of these patterns for the production of written material will much longer survive. The device which will change all this is the word processor.

Present word processors are rather similar in appearance to VDU computer terminals: they comprise a television-style screen and a keyboard. By typing a sentence on the keyboard it can be displayed on the screen, and the area is such that the equivalent of, say, half of one A4 page of manuscript may be seen. Words, lines, even paragraphs can easily be deleted, moved or substituted by simple keyboard operations. As new lines of text are 'typed' at the foot, the whole text rolls up, so that lines progressively vanish at the top. They are not, of course, lost but simply transferred to the backing store of the computer which is at the heart of the word processor. Thus at any time the whole text is available — the display can be 'rolled down' to any desired extent to permit study of earlier parts. A multiplicity of 'type faces' can also be called up to facilitate the inclusion of mathematics. More sophisticated versions may be connected to a document scanner, so that diagrams (at present limited to line diagrams) or facsimiles of other documents can be interpolated in the text being generated.

Thus the word processor makes it possible to generate an extended written work and hold it in the computer store. In this form it can be reviewed, cut, transposed, just as could a copy on paper, but quicker, more conveniently and without the deterioration in image quality which would follow from repeated erasures and substitutions. To put it in another way, a 'scissors-and-paste' compilation can be made without scissors and paste, and with invisible joins in the resulting material. No more need every redraft mean a

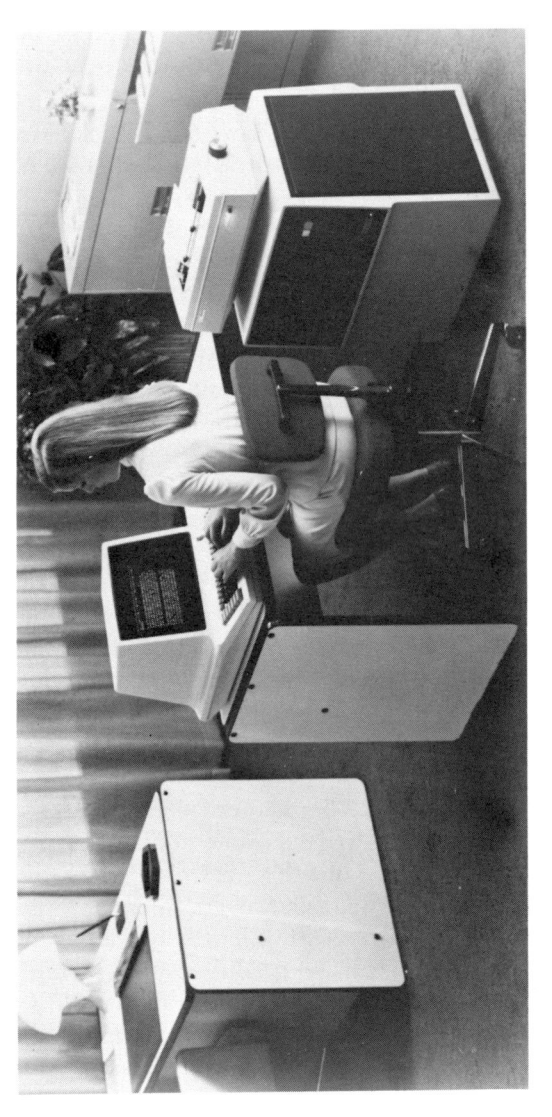

Figure 8: A word-processor, the child of television and the microcomputer, is likely to change profoundly education, clerical work, and creative writing. With it, a civilization based on paper gives way to one based on electronics and telecommunications. (Photograph reproduced by permission of Philips Business Equipment Division.)

re-type. Quickly and expeditiously it can be worked and re-worked until the author is satisfied with it.

However, at this point it exists only within the word processor memory. It can escape from the machine, though, in a number of ways. The most obvious is that the word processor can command an automatic typewriter or line printer to produce hard copy on paper. The outcome will be rather better in quality than present typewritten material. Quite apart from being free from erasures and errors, the word processor will handle the pagination, ensuring that each page contains a precisely equal number of lines, and will justify the text to get rid of the ugly ragged margin on the right-hand side. In short, the gulf of quality between typewritten and printed material will close. The earliest consequence will surely be a growth in technical books and journals based on direct lithographic reproduction of word processor output, generated directly by the author. This is already happening.

The word processor can also give its output on a magnetic record, and perhaps later will do so on a holographic film. In this way the work can be reproduced, either as a display or as hard copy, on any other word processor or at some later date. Finally, the text could be transmitted, perhaps by glass fibre, without intermediate recording, to the internal store of any word processor in the world, for display or reproduction there, or to an archival store, to be held for later retrieval. The words of power will be assembled, stored, conveyed and presented to the eye of the reader, in this last case all entirely without writing or printing: no paper will be involved and the forests of Canada can sleep still their immemorial sleep.

The first word processors in education will appear in the office, large and desk-bound, but even here they will wreak a revolution. For one thing, the secretary will become a personal assistant, colleague, deputy, but will be liberated from copy-typing drudgery. Some will be unable to make the change, but those who do should find their jobs vastly improved. Secondly, the productivity of everybody who works with words should immeasurably increase — not in regard to volume, for that would be a mixed blessing — but rather in the ease with which the text can be revised, reviewed, corrected and updated. The quality of writing will no longer be limited by the fatigue of its improvement.

But a still greater revolution will come a little later, when the word processor becomes a pocket device. For this we shall have to wait for one further innovation, as yet hidden in the womb of time. We need a display device less bulky, capable of better resolution and less greedy of power than the cathode ray tube. A great deal of effort, all around the world, is going into its evolution. The first goal of this research is, of course, a flat-screen television, which could hang on the wall like a picture. For that there would be an enormous market. But just as important would be the effect of the invention of such a display device on the word processor. From something the size of a computer terminal it would be reduced to something the size of, say, a book, suitable to be carried in the hand or the briefcase. Indeed, pocket word processors are already in existence, but they display only a single line of type and this is not enough for adequate editorial purposes. We must await the new display devices in order to be able to see two or three paragraphs presented at once.

When we have this, to notepad and pencil I shall bid my farewell. The battery-powered portable word processor will consume my thoughts, only to pass them electronically to its big brother in the office, where they will be beaten into more elegant form and committed to paper, magnetic tape or such other medium as I may choose. Probably two types of portable word processor will exist: for me there will be one with an alphanumeric keyboard on which I can peck out my prose in a one-fingered way, much as I now use my calculator, slowly, it is true, but faster than I wield a pen, and at a speed commensurate with creative thought. My secretary will scorn such devices. Her word processor will have only a dozen or so keys and she, far better trained than I, will use all the fingers of one hand to key in text faster than it can be spoken. To this shorthand will have come.

In that day, will the printed book survive as we know it? Or will authors simply transmit their work to an archival store from which it may be accessed and reproduced by readers as and when they will? Perhaps the publisher, as we know him, will disappear, at least for scientific and learned books. At present his role is to consider the author's work and make a judgement as to how many the proposed book is likely to sell. He takes quite a large financial risk to launch the books he favours in return for a share of the profit on successful ones. He also provides all the stages of book preparation that lie between manuscript and printer.

In the academic world of the future, the cost of storing a book in the holographic archival stores will be less than the present-day cost of printing and binding a single volume. Many readers will never want a printed copy: if they do, xerography will accomplish it.

Will the publisher then disappear? More probably he will become an archival store keeper. He will accept manuscripts virtually without restriction, hold them in his store, and make a profit from those who call for them, charging a toll: so much for an electronic consultation and so much more for hard copy. In this context, the printer as such will no longer be needed. The publisher's principal problem will be to know what is in his store and make potential readers aware of it: this task of marketing will not be altogether an unfamiliar one.

As to the universities and polytechnics of the future, will their libraries become places where the student goes to consult word processors linked to an archival store where the 'books' are held? Or will the word processors be spread among the departmental buildings, with the library reduced to an archival store, to which hardly anybody ever goes? Or, again, will the students carry portable word processors which they 'charge' with the book they wish to study at the moment, over a line from the library or via a library magnetic tape? I must confess that at this point my wild talents fail me, and my crystal ball clouds over.

Add to all of this the fact that alternatively to nearly half a million books, the million megabit archival store could also hold perhaps thirteen years of continuous, twenty-four-hours-per-day spoken voice, or possibly four months of continuous colour video, using modern coding techniques, and none of us dare begin to say what the consequences of this new technology will be for education, or indeed for any other facet of life in the years to come. What is sobering is that we are concerned here not with the technology of some science fiction twenty-first century, but with the eighties and early nineties of the twentieth.

From sand is the silicon microcircuit created, from sand the optical fibre. The most common and worthless material about us, available in inexhaustible quantities, suddenly is transformed to be the key to all our futures, in a world so different from the one we know that merely to turn our minds to it stuns our imaginations. The task of education in helping our kind to make the transition to a new lifestyle is one which will demand all our skills, insights, flexibility. Yet the role of education is central, for it is in the mind of man that the revolution to come will be fought. In the kingdom of sand all things become possible, and only imagination rules.